Earth's Precious Resources

Plants

A resource our world depends on

Heinemann
LIBRARY

Ian Graham

www.heinemann.co.uk/library

Visit our website to find out more information about **Heinemann Library** books.

To order:
- ☎ Phone 44 (0) 1865 888066
- 🖹 Send a fax to 44 (0) 1865 314091
- 💻 Visit the Heinemann Bookshop at www.heinemann.co.uk/library to browse our catalogue and order online.

First published in Great Britain by Heinemann Library, Halley Court, Jordan Hill, Oxford OX2 8EJ, part of Harcourt Education.
Heinemann is a registered trademark of Harcourt Education Ltd.

Editorial: Andrew Farrow and Dan Nunn
Design: David Poole and Paul Myerscough
Picture Research: Melissa Allison and Andrea Sadler
Production: Duncan Gilbert

Originated by Ambassador Litho Ltd
Printed in China by WKT Company Limited

ISBN 0 431 11551 6
08 07 06 05 04
10 9 8 7 6 5 4 3 2 1

British Library Cataloguing in Publication Data
Graham, Ian
  Plants: a resource our world depends on. – (Earth's precious resources)
  1. Plants, useful – Juvenile literature
  2. Human – plant relationships – Juvenile literature
  I. Title
  581.6
A full catalogue record for this book is available from the British Library.

Acknowledgements
The publishers would like to thank the following for permission to reproduce photographs: Corbis pp. **5 bottom**, **21** (Tom Bean), **27 bottom** (Michael Pole); Ecoscene pp. **5 top** (Papilio Neil Miller), **7 bottom** (Tony Page), **9 top** (Anthony Cooper), **12** (Joel Creed), **24** (Alan Towse), **25** (Andrew Brown), **27 top** (Simon Grove), **28** (Andy Hibbert); FLPA pp. **4** (W. Broadhurst), **6** (Jurgen & Christine Johns), **10** (Hans Dieter Brandl), **11** (Catherine Mullen), **13 top** (D. Hall), **16** (J. Watkins), **20 bottom** (D. Warren), **26** (Maurice Nimmo); Getty Images/Photodisc pp. **9 bottom**; Mary Evans Picture Library p. **13 bottom**; NHPA p. **19** (Stephen Dalton); Royal Botanical Gardens, Kew p. **29**; Science Photo Library pp. **7 top** (Jeremy Walker), **8** (Sidney Moulds), **14** (Alex Barter), **15** (Herman Eisenbess), **18** (Geoff Tompkinson), **20 top** (Simon Fraser), **22 inset**, **23**; Topham Picturepoint p. **17**.

Cover photograph reproduced with permission of Corbis/First Light.

Every effort has been made to contact copyright holders of any material reproduced in this book. Any omissions will be rectified in subsequent printings if notice is given to the publishers.

The paper used to print this book comes from sustainable resources.

Contents

Any words appearing in the text in bold, **like this**, are explained in the Glossary.

What are plants?

Plants are living things that grow in gardens and wild places. Some of them coat the ground and walls with a green carpet, while others stand up above the ground. Plants can be so small that you cannot see them, or they can be trees as big as a tall building. **Stems** or wooden trunks hold their leaves up in the sunshine. Under the ground, their **roots** grow down into the soil and hold them firmly in place.

Why are most plants green?

The green parts of trees and other plants use sunlight to change simple materials from the soil and the air into food. This **process** is called **photosynthesis**. The substance in plants that makes photosynthesis happen is called chlorophyll. Sunlight contains all the colours of the rainbow. Chlorophyll soaks up some but reflects others, mainly green. That is why most plants are green. Red plants have chlorophyll too, but it is masked by other colours.

Plants of all shapes and sizes cover the ground.

Did you know?

Some plants get extra food by catching insects. The plant juices dissolve the trapped insects and the plant takes in the nutritious liquid.

The Venus Fly Trap lives on insects, which it catches by snapping its pair of leaves together.

Fungi

Some things we think of as plants are actually **fungi**. They live on dead and rotting plants, or they suck ready-made food out of living plants. Because fungi do not use sunlight to make food, they have no chlorophyll and so they are not green. Fungi include mushrooms and toadstools, as well as moulds.

Why are plants important?

Plants are vital for life. When green plants use **photosynthesis** to make food, they take in carbon dioxide gas from the atmosphere and give out **oxygen**. The oxygen becomes part of the air around us. People and other animals breathe the air in, take in the oxygen and breathe out carbon dioxide.

Why do we eat plants?

Animals, including humans, cannot make food for themselves in the way that plants do, so we let plants make it and then we eat the plants. Luckily for us, plants make more food than they actually need. They store the extra food in their **roots**, **stems**, **seeds** or fruit. Potatoes, carrots, peas and apples are all examples of food stores in plants that we can eat.

Did you know?

A lot of plants are poisonous and must not be eaten! If you don't know what a plant is, don't eat it!

Most animals depend on plants for food. They either eat plants or eat the animals that live on plants.

What are plants used for?

Plants have a great variety of uses, as well as giving us food. They contain fibres that can be woven into textiles (material) for clothes. For example, cotton comes from the cotton plant, and linen from the flax plant. Canvas is made from cotton or jute. Sisal, from the agave plant, and jute fibres are also used to make ropes. Some medicines are made from substances **extracted** from plants. Timber, from tree trunks, is an essential building material. It is used for building because it is strong and also easy to cut and shape. Plants can even supply fuel for engines.

One of the most widespread and important uses of plants is for food, like the wheat in the photo above.

Bamboo

One of the most useful plants is a type of grass called bamboo. Its **seeds** and **shoots** are eaten. Paper can be made from it. The biggest plants have thick, pipe-like **stems**, strong enough to be used for building.

Forests of fast-growing trees are specially grown to supply timber to the construction **industry**.

How are plants used in medicine?

People have known for thousands of years that some plants could ease their health problems. Treating illnesses with plants is called herbal medicine. Herbal medicine is still widely used today. Some modern medicines also use plants, but the medicines are produced by scientific methods. Aspirin was one of the first modern medicines, and it is still a commonly used painkiller today. The painkilling chemical in aspirin comes from willow trees. Penicillin, a medicine that kills some disease **organisms**, comes from a mould, a type of **fungus**.

Some medicines are made from moulds that grow on stale food.

How do plants keep us healthy?

A good diet contains everything we need to stay healthy. Small amounts of substances called vitamins and minerals are essential. Some of these come from meat and dairy products, but many of them come from fruits, vegetables and **cereals**. Plants also give us fibre, or roughage. This gives the muscles inside us something to push against, so they can move food through our body.

What are flowers used for?

We use flowers for many of the ceremonies that mark important events, especially weddings and funerals. Vases of flowers also brighten people's homes and offices. Growing flowers to meet this demand is a huge business in some countries, especially the USA, the Netherlands and Japan. The Netherlands is world-famous for its tulip crops. Cold storage and fast air transport enable growers to send fresh flowers all over the world within a day or two.

Flower markets supply a great variety of flowers from all over the world.

Did you know?

Saffron is one of the most expensive spices used in cooking. It is made from part of the crocus flower. About 170,000 flowers have to be picked by hand to produce just 1 kilogram (2.2 pounds) of saffron!

Why are plants good for the land?

As trees and other plants grow, their **roots** spread through the ground and help to stop the soil from being blown or washed away. Road and railway embankments are planted with grass to hold the soil together.

Coastal erosion

Coastal erosion occurs when the wind and the sea wear away part of the coast. It can be reduced by planting grass along the seashore. Most grass will not live in sand with salty water splashing them. However, a type of grass called marram grass, or beach grass, can live in sand near the sea. As well as roots, this tough grass has underground stems that can grow up to 15 metres (50 feet) long and send up shoots at intervals. The network of stems and roots helps to hold the sand together.

Marram grass holds sand dunes together.

What is biomass?

Biomass fuel is made from plant and animal waste. Trees and other green plants take in energy from the Sun all through their lives. We use this energy by burning the plants. The energy stored inside them changes into heat and light.

Biomass fuel was the only fuel that people could burn to cook food and warm themselves for thousands of years. It is still the main fuel used in most parts of the developing world. Today, we have **fossil fuels**, including coal, oil and natural gas, but these fuels will not last forever. Biomass fuel is a renewable energy source – it can be regrown and so it will not run out. Biomass fuel is therefore now being burned in some power stations to make electricity.

Wood has been used as a fuel for fires for thousands of years.

How can plants power cars?

Plants contain starch and sugar, which can be **processed** to make other substances. One of these substances, ethanol, can be burned in an engine instead of petrol. It can also be added to other fuels to make them last longer. A mixture of petrol and ethanol is called gasohol. Countries with little or no oil of their own are interested in using ethanol to reduce their energy costs. They can grow plants to make fuel instead of having to buy it all.

A gas called hydrogen can also be made from plants and it, too, can be burned in engines. Today, hydrogen is made from natural gas. In future, when natural gas has run out, we may start growing forests and crops such as sugar beet to make fuel for cars.

This gasohol station is located in Brazil.

How do trees make parties more fun?

Party balloons are made from a natural rubber called latex, which comes from trees. When the bark of a rubber tree is cut, milky **sap** called latex oozes out. It is collected and used to make things, including party balloons.

Party balloons and surgical gloves are made from latex from rubber trees.

How are the colours in plants used?

The stems, leaves, roots and fruits of some trees and other plants are strongly coloured. They can be used as natural dyes to colour cloth. Nettle leaves produce a green dye. Dark blue berries from the elder plant produce a blue dye. A black dye can be made from the bark of the alder tree. A red dye can be made from meadowsweet root.

Did you know?

In ancient Britain, warriors painted their bodies with a blue dye called woad, from the woad plant, before they went into battle.

Where are plants found?

Plants are found nearly everywhere on Earth. Most plants grow best in certain conditions. Cacti grow best in dry conditions. Seaweed and other aquatic plants grow underwater. Alpines are best suited to high, cold places. Bog plants do well in waterlogged soil. There are plants for almost every type of habitat (natural home for a plant or animal) on Earth.

A place where similar plants live in similar conditions is called a biome, or major life zone. A tropical **rainforest** is one biome. Desert is another biome.

Cacti can live in ground that is too dry for most plants.

Did you know?

Trees live the longest of all plants. Most oak trees live up to 300 years, but some have lived for 1500 years. Giant sequoia trees can live 2500 years. The oldest living plant on Earth is a bristlecone pine tree in California, USA, that is over 4765 years old.

Do all plants grow in soil?

Most plants grow in soil, but a lot of plants can grow in places where there is no soil. Lichens grow on rock. They take in water and **nutrients** from the rain that falls on them. Mistletoe grows on trees. Its **roots** grow into the tree and suck water and food out. Mosses grow in damp places, even if there is no soil. Plants called bromeliads can grow high up in the tree-tops of rainforests, perched on the sides of trees.

Did you know?

Some plants help each other! Orchid plants have a **fungus** living on their roots. Orchids are not very good at making food for themselves. The fungus does it for them. In return, the orchid provides a home for the fungus. This partnership between different living things is called symbiosis.

How do plants spread?

Flowering plants, including trees, multiply by producing **seeds**, which grow into new plants. Tiny particles called pollen are produced by the male parts of the flower. They are carried away by insects or on the wind. Some of them land on other flowers and join with the flowers' female parts. Together, they grow into seeds. Many plants are also able to grow a whole new plant from part of their own **stem** or root.

Some seeds are small enough to blow away on the wind. Others are eaten by birds. Seeds often pass through birds undamaged and, later, drop to the ground. Some seeds stick to the coats of passing animals, which carry them away. In this way, new plants can grow a long way from their parent plants.

Trees produce new trees by making seeds, like these seeds on a sycamore tree.

How are plants processed?

Plants are often used just as they are, straight from nature. They are also **processed** in lots of different ways. The fruits and vegetables they produce are peeled, boiled, roasted and pressed to make a variety of foods and drinks. Wheat grain is ground to produce flour for making bread. Heating hard vegetables such as potatoes and carrots makes them softer and easier to eat. Boiling them also kills any germs that might be on them. Fruits, such as oranges and pineapples, are pressed to squeeze the juice out for making fruit drinks. Tea is made from dried leaves and coffee is made by roasting beans from coffee bushes.

Fibres are **extracted** from plants for making paper and textiles. Plants are also treated with chemicals to make special ingredients for medicines.

Cooking softens hard vegetables and kills germs.

CASE STUDY:
Papermaking

Paper for newspapers, magazines, books, writing pads, envelopes, tissues and toilet paper is made from trees. First, tree trunks are chopped up. Then they are ground into a thick porridge-like material called pulp. The pulp may be bleached to stop the paper from turning yellow. A papermaking machine spreads the watery pulp onto a moving belt. The belt is made from a mesh with holes in it. Water drains out through the holes. The mat of fibres passes between rollers, which squeeze out more water. Then hot rollers dry it out and polished rollers smooth it. The paper comes out of the machine and is wound into giant rolls.

Did you know?

A papermaking machine can make more than 30 metres (100 feet) of paper a second.

There is a constant need for wood from trees to make paper.

How can plants be harmed?

Plants can be harmed by many things, including insects and other animals, the weather and some substances given out by traffic and **industry**. And, just like you, plants can catch diseases that can harm or even kill them. They can also be harmed by people trampling over them or collecting plants from nature.

How do insects harm plants?

Lots of insects and other creatures want the food that plants make. Insects such as locusts eat the whole plant. Other insects bite into plants and suck out their watery **sap**. In nature, plants and their insect pests live in balance with each other. Even if insects do not kill a plant, the damage they do can let in other **organisms**, such as **bacteria**, **viruses** and **fungi**. Farmers try to reduce the damage pests cause by treating crops with materials called pesticides that kill pests.

Aphids are plant pests that feed by sucking the watery sap out of plants.

How does acid rain harm plants?

Gases produced by engines and some power stations join with moisture in the air and form harmful substances called acids. When it rains, the rain is acid. When acid rain falls on plants, it damages the sensitive tips of their **shoots** and **roots**. It also damages their leaves and lets disease organisms in. Acid rain falling over a wide area can harm a whole forest.

These trees have been damaged by acid rain.

How does weather affect plants?

Trees and other plants can be harmed by bad weather. Strong winds can blow trees over. A great storm that swept across England in 1987 uprooted 15 million trees! Frost can damage tender buds of new leaves and flowers that are beginning to grow. Heavy rain can flatten crops. Most plants depend on a constant supply of water, so **drought** can be disastrous for them.

Plants are easily damaged or destroyed by extreme weather.

CASE STUDY:
America's prairies

North America once had vast grasslands called prairies. They covered large parts of the continent and stretched as far as the eye could see. They were created by **droughts**, grazing animals, and fires that stopped trees from growing and forming forests. The land, plants, animals and **native American** people lived together in a natural balance. Then European settlers arrived. They turned the **fertile** prairie land into farmland, stopped the fires and killed many of the grazing animals. Almost all of the prairies were destroyed.

Now, some prairies are being recreated. The **native** prairie plant **species** are being re-planted and animals are grazing on the land again. One advantage of restoring prairie land is that, unlike farmland, it does not need chemicals to control weeds or insect pests.

North America was once covered by prairies like this.

21

What are genetically modified plants?

Trees and other plants are made of cells. Most plant cells are too small to see without a microscope. Every cell contains a set of instructions that tell the plant how to grow. The instructions are called **genes** and all the genes together are called the genetic code, or genome. It is this code that makes one **seed** grow into a grass plant and another grow into an oak tree.

Scientists have learned how to read the genes in a plant's cells. They have also learned how to change them. A plant with genes that have been changed by scientists is called a genetically modified **organism**, or GMO.

Plants are made from cells.

Why do scientists change plant genes?

Traditionally, plant breeders produce plants by getting them to make seeds and then growing the seeds. By breeding only from the biggest plants, however, the breeders can produce plants that are bigger. Similarly, by breeding only from plants that produce very large crops of fruit, they can grow new plants that produce even better crops. This is called selective breeding, because the growers select, or choose, which plants to breed from.

Some scientists try to understand which of a plant's genes make it bigger or produce more fruit or make it resist diseases. If they know this, they can change the genes and produce exactly the plants that they want. Changing a plant's genes is called **genetic engineering**.

Scientists can take genes from one plant and put them in a different plant.

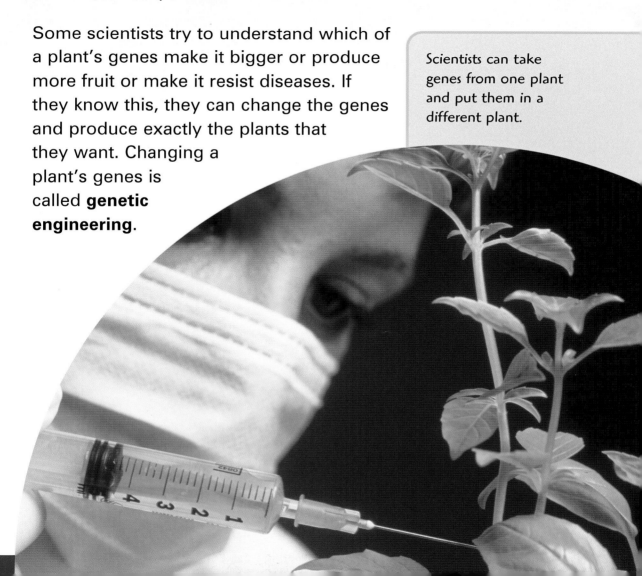

Is genetic engineering good or bad?

Some people think changing plants by genetic engineering is a good thing. Others are just as sure it is a bad thing.

In favour of genetic engineering

Scientists want to improve plants to feed more people. For example, scientists have produced a new type of rice that grows well in cold weather and in drier, salty soil. This rice can feed people in places where rice normally does not grow well. Other plants are being improved in the same way.

Against genetic engineering

Some people fear that new genes being put into crops will spread into wild plants and change them too. They fear that changing plant genes in unnatural ways could produce super-weeds that are hard to kill.

Some people feel so strongly about genetic engineering that they protest against it.

CASE STUDY:
GM crops in Mexico

Some farmers, especially those who run **organic farms**, choose not to grow genetically modified (GM) crops. They want their crops to be completely natural without any **genes** that have been changed by **genetic engineering**. In a part of Mexico called Oaxaca, there are thousands of small farms growing just enough food for the families that farm the land. When the corn grown on these farms was tested, some of it was found to be genetically modified.

Scientists think GM corn from the USA that was meant to be eaten might have been grown instead. Genes from the GM corn would then have spread to other corn plants as they bred together and made new **seeds** and new corn plants. Once genes from genetically modified plants are released in to nature they cannot then be taken back into the laboratory.

This field of GM corn is in Illinois, USA. Some GM plants have already spread their genes to wild plants.

Will plants ever disappear?

Plants are so good at finding places to live that they will probably never disappear altogether. However, some types of plant can die out, or become extinct. We know this has happened already, because we can find traces of plants that grew long ago, but are not found anywhere today. If one type of plant disappears, it can affect a whole **ecosystem** – a community of plants and animals, and the place where they live. Some of the tiny creatures that live on the plants may die out and the larger creatures that live on them may not have enough to eat.

Scientists believe there are many plant **species** that have not been discovered yet, especially in places like the Amazon **rainforest**. Some of them may contain substances of great value to medicine. These plants may be disappearing because of forest clearance without us ever knowing about them.

Fossils show us that many species of plants have died out in the past.

Why are forests at risk?

Trees are cut down in great numbers to clear land for farming and to supply wood for the construction, furniture and paper **industries**. If old, slow-growing trees are felled, it takes so long for new trees to grow that the forest may not recover. **Rainforests** are being cut down at an amazing rate. An area the size of the UK is cut down every year. Replanting projects try to replace these trees. However, new forests are often planted using only one or two tree **species** instead of the great variety of trees and other plants that grew in the original forest.

Rainforests are the world's oldest **ecosystems**. This one is in Australia.

Did you know?

Most of New Zealand's **native** forests were cut down to clear the land for farming. Today, the remaining native forests are protected and pine forests are grown to supply the timber industry.

How can we look after trees and plants?

There are lots of ways to look after plants. One way is to stay on paths in the countryside instead of walking over wild flowers. Reducing **air pollution** would cause less acid rain and so reduce the damage it causes to plants. Strict control of logging (cutting down trees) and land clearance would help to protect forests. We can also make sure that the wood products we buy come from sustainable forests. These are forests that provide a continuing supply of timber.

We can replant trees and other plants that are at risk. Most countries now have national parks where native trees and other plants are protected.

Why do some plants have to be controlled?

Plants are sometimes brought into a country where they do not normally grow. If the conditions are ideal, they grow so strongly that they smother other plants. For example, about 300 native plants in the USA are threatened by plants introduced from somewhere else.

Giant hogweed is a problem plant in Britain.

CASE STUDY:
The Millennium Seed Bank Project

The Millennium **Seed** Bank Project is an international effort to prevent 24,000 plant **species** from around the world from dying out and disappearing forever. The seeds of these plants are being collected and stored. If the plants die out in nature, the stored seeds can be grown and the plants put back in nature.

Seeds are sent to the project's headquarters in England, where they are cleaned and checked to make sure they are healthy. They are then dried and frozen at −20 °C (−4 °F). Every 10 years, some of the seeds are taken out of storage and grown to check that they are still alive.

Seeds of endangered plants are collected and stored carefully for the future.

Glossary

air pollution harmful or poisonous substances in the air

bacteria tiny organisms made of just one cell

cereal any type of grass that produces starchy seeds that can be eaten

drought dry period that lasts longer than normal

ecosystem all the plants and animals that live in a place, together with their surroundings

extract take something out of something else

fertile having all the nutrients necessary to produce healthy plant growth

fossil remains of a plant (or animal) that lived millions of years ago

fossil fuel a fuel made from the remains of living things, such as coal, oil or natural gas

fungus (plural is fungi) type of living thing, including mushrooms and toadstools, that feeds on plants or animals

genes pieces of a substance called DNA that contain the instructions for making a plant (or animal)

genetic engineering changing a living thing's genetic code

industry businesses that extract and process materials and make goods

native something that has lived in a place for a very long time and has not been brought in from somewhere else

native Americans people who first lived in America before European settlers arrived

nutrients substances taken in by plants and used for growth

organic farm farm where plants or animals are looked after using natural methods

organisms living plants or animals

oxygen gas in the air that green plants produce during photosynthesis

photosynthesis using light to make something. In plants, photosynthesis produces food from the soil and air.

process to treat a material in a particular way, so it can be used for something

rainforest thick forest in hot parts of the world that have very high rainfall

root part of a plant that grows underground, taking up water and nutrients from the soil

sap watery substance found inside plants. Sap contains nutrients from the roots and sugary food made in the leaves.

seed part of a plant that grows into a new plant

shoots baby leaves or branches

species group of related plants (or animals)

stem part of a plant above the ground that holds the leaves

virus tiny organism that reproduces inside cells and causes illness

Find out more

Books

How Flowers Grow, Angela Wilkes (Usborne Publishing, 2003)

Kingfisher Pocket Guide: Trees, David Sutton (Kingfisher Books, 2002)

Nature's Mysteries: How Plants Grow, Malcolm Penny
   (Franklin Watts, 2003)

Oxford First Encyclopedia: Animals and Plants, Andrew Langley
   (Oxford University Press, 2002)

Science, the Facts: Flowering Plants, Rebecca Hunter
   (Franklin Watts, 2003)

Trees and Plants: Rainforests, Edward Parker (Hodder Wayland, 2002)

Websites

www.nbii.gov/disciplines/botany/science.html

Lots of information, projects, science and games about trees and plants of all sorts from the US National Biological Information Infrastructure.

www.fs.fed.us/kids

Smokey Bear and Woodsy Owl's guide to looking after forests, from the US Department of Agriculture Forest Service.

www.ars.usda.gov/is/kids/plants/plantsintro.htm

Information about plants from the US Department of Agriculture's Agricultural Research Service.

www.forestry.gov.uk/forestry/infd-5pzffm

A useful 'Forest Factfile' from the UK Forestry Commission.

Disclaimer

All the Internet addresses (URLs) given in this book were valid at the time of going to press. However, due to the dynamic nature of the Internet, some addresses may have changed, or sites may have ceased to exist since publication. While the author and publishers regret any inconvenience this may cause readers, no responsibility for any such changes can be accepted by either the author or the publishers.

Index

Titles in the *Earth's Precious Resources* series include:

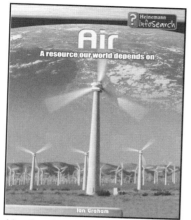

Hardback   0 431 11556 7

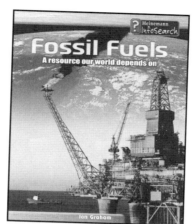

Hardback   0 431 11550 8

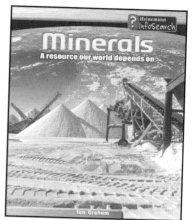

Hardback   0 431 11552 4

Hardback   0 431 11551 6

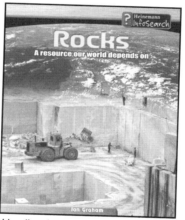

Hardback   0 431 11553 2

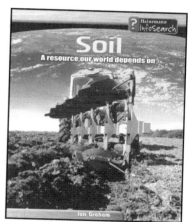

Hardback   0 431 11554 0

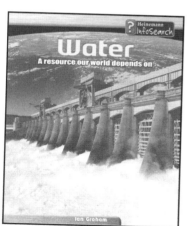

Hardback   0 431 11555 9

Find out about the other titles in this series on our website www.heinemann.co.uk/library